What a Shop!

CONTENTS

NATIONAL GEOGRAPHIC School Publishing
Hampton-Brown

Words with wh

Look at each picture. Read the words.

Example:

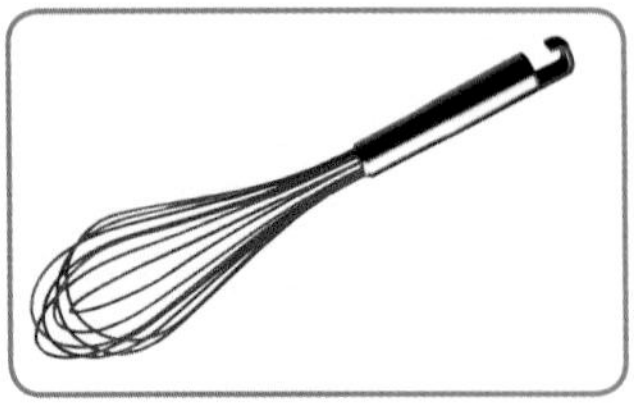

whisk

whack

whip

wham

High Frequency Words
come
found
full
next
their
walk

Key Words

Look at the picture.

Read the sentences.

A Ball Is Found

1. Sam and Lin **walk** every day.
2. One day they **found** a ball!
3. It is **full** of air that won't **come** out.
4. What will they find on **their next walk**?

GO! Phonics Games
NGReach.com

Rubber

by Dee Wallis

Their tub ducks are rubber. What is rubber? Where is it from?

Rubber comes from a tree! A worker cuts a slit in a tree. What will come out?

A worker adds a tap and a cup, then walks to the next tree and cuts it.

The rubber does not whiz out. It fills the cups drop by drop.

When a cup is full, the rubber is put in a tank truck.

The truck is sent to a factory. Can you get a whiff of the rubber?

Lots of things are rubber! Which things do you have?

Words with wh

Read these words.

whack	bath	wham	bat	which
duck	whiff	froth	whip	whisk

Find the words with **wh**.
Use letters to build them.

w h i c h

Talk Together

Use the whisk for a froth.

What can you use these rubber things for? Use words from the box above to tell your partner.

1.

2.

3.

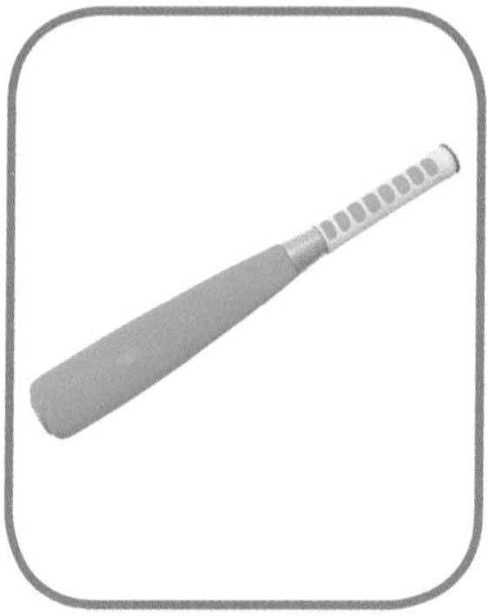

Words with **sh**

Look at the pictures. Read the words.

Example:

shell

bru**sh**

fi**sh**

tra**sh**

shelf

ship

High Frequency **Words**

High Frequency Words
come
found
full
next
their
walk

Key Words

Look at the pictures. Read the sentences.

The Shell Shop

1. **Their** shop is **full** of shells!
2. **Come** and **walk** in the shop with me.
3. Have you **found** a shell to buy?
4. What shell will we see **next**?

Phonics Games
NGReach.com

Let's Shop!

by Kelsey Bruce

A shop can be a shack, a shed, or a big building. Come and see!

This is a shop. It is full of clothes.

You can get a silk sash.

This is a shop. It is full of dishes.

You can get a mug.

This is a shop. It is full of beach things. You can get a shell.

This is a shop. It is full of fresh fish. You can get a crab.

This is a shop. It is full of masks. You can get one.

What have you found out? Where would you like to shop next? ❖

Words with sh

Read these words.

big	brush	fish	flash
little	shed	shell	ship

Find the words with **sh**.
Use letters to build them.

f l a s h

Talk Together

Choose words from the box above to tell your partner what you see in the shops.

I see a shed at the big shop.

What a Mess!

This kitchen is a mess! Help Trish and Josh figure out how to clean it up. Take turns reading the clues.

1. Where does the bag full of trash go?
2. On which shelf do the mugs go?
3. Trish found their big dish rag, but where is their whisk?
4. Where is a brush for scrubbing a dish?
5. When ants come, what will they eat?

Acknowledgments
Grateful acknowledgment is given to the authors, artists, photographers, museums, publishers, and agents for permission to reprint copyrighted material. Every effort has been made to secure the appropriate permission. If any omissions have been made or if corrections are required, please contact the Publisher.

Photographic Credits
CVR (Cover) Kunst & Scheidulin/Pixtal/age fotostock. **2** (b) Rob Friedman/iStockphoto. (r) Bratwustle/Shutterstock. (t) Sergei Didyk/Shutterstock. **3** (b) Liz Garza Williams/Hampton-Brown/National Geographic School Publishing. **4** (b) Emin Ozkan/Shutterstock. (t) LM Productions/Getty Images. **5** Peter & Georgina Bowater/Stock Connection. **6-7** Justin Guariglia/National Geographic Image Collection. **7** (inset) Ed Morris/Getty Images. **8** STR New/Reuters. **9** Maggie Janik/Photographers Direct. **10** (bc) DNY59/iStockphoto. (bl) Jerome Skiba/iStockphoto. (br) ANDREASBELIAS/iStockphoto. (cc) design56/iStockphoto. (cl) Igor Terekhov/iStockphoto. (cr) Marie-france Bélanger/iStockphoto. (tc) JR Trice/iStockphoto. (tl) Ana Amorim/iStockphoto. (tr) aguirre_mar/iStockphoto. **11** (bc) Mark Cinotti/Shutterstock. (bl) Laurence Mouton/PhotoAlto/Corbis. (br) Mark Thiessen/Hampton-Brown/National Geographic School Publishing. (t) Liz Garza Williams/Hampton-Brown/National Geographic School Publishing. **12** (bl) moodboard/Veer. (br) howard Oates/iStockphoto. (cl) Ljupco Smokovski/Shutterstock. (cr) Dino O./Shutterstock. (tl) Alex Bramwell/iStockphoto. (tr) HomeStudio/Shutterstock. **13** (b) Liz Garza Williams/Hampton-Brown/National Geographic School Publishing. (t) Images&Stories/Photographers Direct. **14** (b) Steve Vidler/SuperStock. (c) Bill Parsons/Mira.com. (t) Jeff Gynane/Shutterstock. **15** (b) Michael Freeman/Aurora Photos. (t) Photo Japan/Alamy Images. **16** (b) Edie Layland/iStockphoto. (t) Marc Romanelli/Getty Images. **17** (b) yingyang0/iStockphoto. (t) Linda Bucklin/Shutterstock. **18** (b) Kari Høglund/iStockphoto. (t) Anthony Plummer/Lonely Planet Images. **19** (b) Rafael Laguillo/iStockphoto. (t) Luca Tettoni/Corbis. **20** Mirenska Olga/Shutterstock. **21** (t) Liz Garza Williams/Hampton-Brown/National Geographic School Publishing.

Illustrator Credits
3, 21, 22-23 Peter Grosshauser

National Geographic School Publishing
Hampton-Brown
www.NGSP.com

Printed in the USA.
Qaud Graphics, Leominster, MA

ISBN:978-0-7362-8033-4

18 19
10 9 8 7